A Family in France

**A pronunciation guide for the French names
and words used in this book appears on page 28.**

LIBRARY OF CONGRESS CATALOGING IN PUBLICATION DATA

Regan, Mary
   A family in France.

   Summary: Presents the life of a family living in an
apartment in France, describing the work of the parents and
the school and recreational activities of the two boys.
   1. Family—France—Rennes—Juvenile literature.
[1. Family life—France.   2. France—Social life and
customs] I. Fairclough, Chris, i11.   II. Title.
HQ624.R44   1985   306.8'5'094415   84-1392
ISBN 0-8225-1651-9 (lib. bdg.)

Manufactured in the United States of America

   3   4   5   6   7   8   9   10   94   93   92   91   90

A Family in France

Mary Regan

Photographs by Chris Fairclough

Lerner Publications Company · Minneapolis

Pascal Gué is ten years old. He lives in Rennes, a city in the northwest part of France, with his parents and his brother Stéphane, who is eight.

France is divided into ninety-six departments. Rennes is the capital of Ille et Vilaine, one of the four departments in the region of Brittany.

Rennes is a very old city. Downtown in the central business district, where Pascal's father works, there are cobbled streets and houses built with wooden beams.

Toward the outskirts of the city where Pascal lives there are many modern shops, offices, and houses.

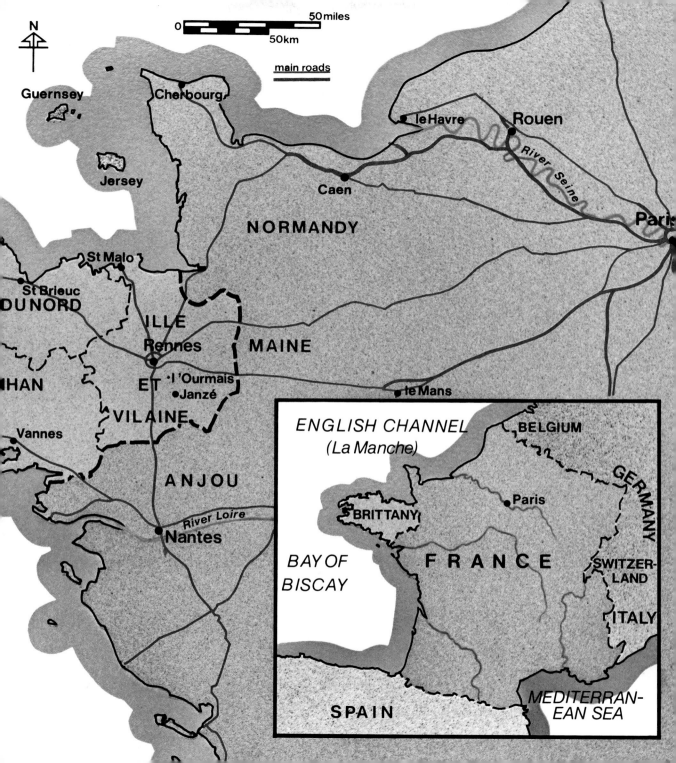

The Gué family lives in an apartment on the fourteenth floor of a high-rise building. There is a very good view from the apartment, but Madame Gué says that she sometimes gets dizzy because it's so high up.

They live in a part of Rennes called Maurepas, about a mile and a half (2½ kilometers) from downtown. It's a fairly new part of the city and is named after the nearby park of Maurepas.

Monsieur Gué is a mail carrier. He works in the largest post office in Rennes. It takes Monsieur Gué about twenty minutes to bicycle to work, and he has to be there by 6:30 in the morning!

Monsieur Gué usually works in the post office until 9:00 A.M. Then he gets on his bicycle and sets off on his route. The letters are kept in leather bags strapped to his bike.

Monsieur Gué knows many of the people on his route. He often stops for a chat with the shopkeepers when he delivers their letters.

If he delivers the mail to an apartment building, Monsieur Gué puts the letters in boxes outside the main door. There is a different box for each apartment.

Sometimes Monsieur Gué has to deliver postal orders. He pays the money directly to the person whose name is on the postal order. Then he asks them to sign a special book to prove that they have received the money. He carries the money in a leather bag which he must always wear over his shoulder.

By mid-morning, Monsieur Gué has delivered all of the letters in his bags. He stops at a special "relay box" to collect the rest of the mail for his route.

9

Monsieur Gué finishes his route at 12:30. He goes back to the post office to sign out and then slowly pedals home.

It's lunchtime, so the streets are very busy. *Agents de police*, or police officers, wear white hats and gloves when they are directing traffic. Rain has been predicted, so this officer also wears a raincoat.

Some of the most colorful parts of the city are the pedestrian areas, where no traffic is allowed. People stroll around and look at the shops. The Place de la Mairie (Town Hall Square) is one of the busiest spots in Rennes. In the square, there are brightly colored flower stalls where many people stop to buy flowers.

There are also cafés. If the weather is nice, people sit at tables outside and have something to eat or drink.

11

Pascal and Stéphane wake up after their father has gone to work. On weekdays, they usually have *café au lait* and bread for breakfast. *Café au lait* is made of coffee and warm milk and is drunk from bowls. On weekends, Madame Gué makes hot chocolate and *croissants* or *pain au chocolat*, a kind of roll with a piece of chocolate in the middle.

School starts at 8:30 in the morning. Pascal and Stéphane both go to the Saint Laurent primary school. It's just down the road, so they walk there together.

This is Pascal's last year at primary school. Next year, he will go to the *lycée*, or secondary school. There are thirty-two children in his class. Their teacher, Madame Ségalen, is also the principal of the school.

Pascal's class has elected a group of monitors to keep the classroom clean and tidy. The monitors have a meeting every week. Pascal is the blackboard monitor. He leads today's meeting, but Madame Ségalen stays in the classroom to make sure it doesn't get too noisy.

Madame Gué starts work as soon as the children have gone to school. Twice a week, she helps some friends with their fruit and vegetable stall at the market in Maurepas. In early summer, there are many kinds of fresh fruits and vegetables. The market is very busy. Madame Gué's stall is piled high with asparagus, green beans, tomatoes, and fruit such as cherries, strawberries, and peaches.

When Madame Gué has finished work, she buys some food at the market and hurries home to make lunch. Pascal and Stéphane have their lunch break from 11:30 A.M. to 1:00 P.M. Because they live nearby, they go home for lunch.

In France, lunch is the most important meal of the day. Most people have a long lunch break. The Gué family usually has a six-course lunch, including salad, cheese, and dessert. The main course is fish or meat, and the vegetables are eaten as a separate course.

After lunch, the boys have time to do some homework before they go back to school. Stéphane goes to his bedroom to practice the recorder. He has music lessons twice a week, and the teacher always gives his class some tunes to play at home.

Pascal starts his math homework. Math is not his favorite subject. He prefers to write stories, but he needs to work on his French grammar!

Monsieur Gué has finished work for the day. In the afternoon, he does some odd jobs around the house. Some hooks in the bathroom need repairing. The bathtub looks very small because it has a built-in seat so you can sit down in the bath or stand up for a shower.

The family's bicycles need fixing, too. Monsieur Gué repairs all of them himself. Pascal helps when he gets home from school. He's learning to care for his own bike properly.

French children go to school on Saturday mornings and have Wednesday afternoons free. In winter, Pascal and Stéphane ice skate or play football on Wednesday afternoons. French football is the game we call soccer. Sometimes the boys go swimming instead.

On Saturday afternoon, Pascal and Stéphane help their mother with the shopping. Pascal goes to the bakery to buy some bread for the evening meal. The bakery, which sells many kinds of bread in different shapes and sizes, smells delicious inside. Pascal buys a *baguette*, which is a long stick of fresh white bread.

Stéphane and Madame Gué go to the Monoprix, the local supermarket. There Madame Gué buys milk and other items she needs.

Stéphane likes shopping at the market best of all. The stalls sell all kinds of things: herbs, fresh meat and fish, sausage, fruit, and vegetables.

Some stalls even sell live shellfish. Stéphane spends some time watching the crabs scuttle around in their trays.

Further down the marketplace, Madame Gué buys some cheese. There are small packages of white goat's cheese and huge wheels of Brie and Port Salut. Camembert is a popular kind of cheese. It's creamy white inside, with a thick skin. Brie, Port Salut, and Camembert are all made in France.

Like many other French people, the members of the Gué family are Catholic. On Saturday evening, they go to Mass at the Church of Saint Laurent. Father Jean is their priest. He and the people of Maurepas built the church themselves. It's built from stone, timber, mortar, glass, and steel.

Father Jean is a very good friend of the Gué family. After Mass, Monsieur and Madame Gué invite him over for supper and tell him what they have been doing during the week.

This Sunday is Pascal's eleventh birthday. To celebrate, the family is going to the country to see his uncle Hamar, his aunt Thérèse, and his cousins, Sonia and Denis. Monsieur Gué loads the car with fishing rods and baskets of food, and they set off.

Uncle Hamar lives in the village of l'Ourmais, which is about ten miles (15 kilometers) from Rennes. He is very proud of his house, which is 200 years old. When he bought the house, it was in very bad condition. The family has done a lot of work on the house, but they have much left to do.

Hamar was born in Algeria and came to France 15 years ago. He is a Muslim, and Hamar is a Muslim name. His son Denis also has a Muslim name—Ali. He is usually called Denis at school and Ali at home.

Aunt Thérèse makes Breton *galettes* for lunch. *Galettes* are a kind of pancake. They can be eaten many different ways—dipped in buttermilk, filled with ham and eggs, or covered with jam or honey.

After lunch, Hamar takes the children to see his rabbits. They pick up the rabbits and pet them. But Sonia and Denis know that the rabbits are raised to be eaten, so they try not to get too fond of them.

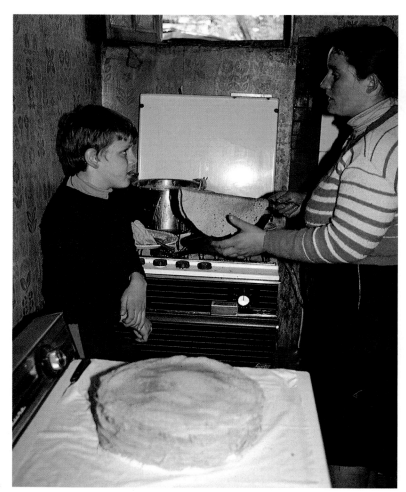

The afternoon is warm and sunny, and the Gué family walks down to the river near Uncle Hamar's house to go fishing. During the summer, they often take a picnic lunch and spend all day by the river.

Today they spend only a few hours on the riverbank, enjoying the sun and the water. They want to return home in time for supper. Soon they say goodbye to their relatives and drive back to Rennes.

At home, Pascal and Stéphane help their mother make supper. In Pascal's honor, they are having a special meal with all kinds of shellfish—crabs, prawns, shrimp, crayfish, oysters, and tiny sea snails. Pascal likes the snails. He fishes them out of the shell with a pin and swallows them whole.

Stéphane asks if he can also have a special meal on his birthday. Madame Gué says she will make one for him on his "name day." In France, a person's name day is as important as a birthday. French people are often named after saints, and each saint has a special feast day. Saint Stephen's Day is on December 26, so Stéphane celebrates his name day then.

At last it's time for the birthday cake. Pascal's cake is called a *vacherin* and is made of blackcurrant ice cream, meringue, and fresh cream. There are eleven candles on the top. Pascal blows them all out at once. The rest of the family sings "Joyeux Anniversaire," which means, of course, "Happy Birthday."

French Words in This Book

agent de police ah-JAHN duh po-LEASE
baguette bah-GET
Brie BREE
café au lait kah-FAY oh LAY
Camembert KAM-mem-behr
croissants kwah-SAWHN
Denis deh-NEE
galette gah-LET
Gué goo-AY
Hamar hah-MAHR
Ille et Vilaine EEL ay vee-LEN
Jean ZHAWN
Joyeux Anniversaire zhwoy-YEUZ a-nee-vair-SARE
l'Ourmais loor-MAY
lycée lee-SAY
Madame mah-DAHM
Maurepas maw-reh-PAH
Monoprix moh-noh-PREE
Monsieur muh-SYEUH
pain au chocolat pan oh sho-koh-LAH
Pascal pah-SKAHL
Place de la Mairie plahss duh lah meh-REE
Port Salut POUR sah-LOO
Rennes REN
Saint Laurent san law-RAWN
Stéphane stay-FAHN
Thérèse tay-REZ
vacherin vah-sheh-RAN

Facts about France

Capital: Paris

Language: French

Form of Money: The French franc

National Holiday: Bastille Day, July 14
This day marks the capture of the
Bastille, a prison in Paris, during the
French Revolution. Bastille Day is
celebrated with parades and fireworks.

Area: 211,208 square miles (547,026 square
kilometers), including the island of
Corsica, which is part of France
France is almost two times the size of
the state of Colorado, or less than one-
tenth the size of the United States, not
counting Alaska or Hawaii.

Population: about 54 million people
The population of France is about one-
fourth the population of the United States.

NORTH
AMERICA

SOUTH
AMERICA

EUROPE

ASIA

France

AFRICA

AUSTRALIA

Families the World Over

Some children in foreign countries live like you do. Others live very differently. In these books, you can meet children from all over the world. You'll learn about their games and schools, their families and friends, and what it's like to grow up in a faraway land.

Lerner Publications Company, 241 First Avenue North, Minneapolis, Minnesota 55401